What We Have in Common

A Brim Coloring Book

Written by Jane Landey
Edited by David Austin
Drawings by David Austin and Jane Austin

Introduction

What We Have in Common. Brim Coloring Books display the similarities of related animals. In this series the crocodile and the alligator are compared. The facts enable children to appreciate common values. Thus, imbibing in them interest towards animals which could make them appreciate what they have in common with one another.

THE CROCODILE

AND

THE ALLIGATOR

The crocodile and the alligator have many things in common.
They look alike and are flesh eaters.
Both live in water.

A crocodile and an alligator meet
on a windy rainy day.

Hello Mister Alligator.

Hello Mister Crocodile.

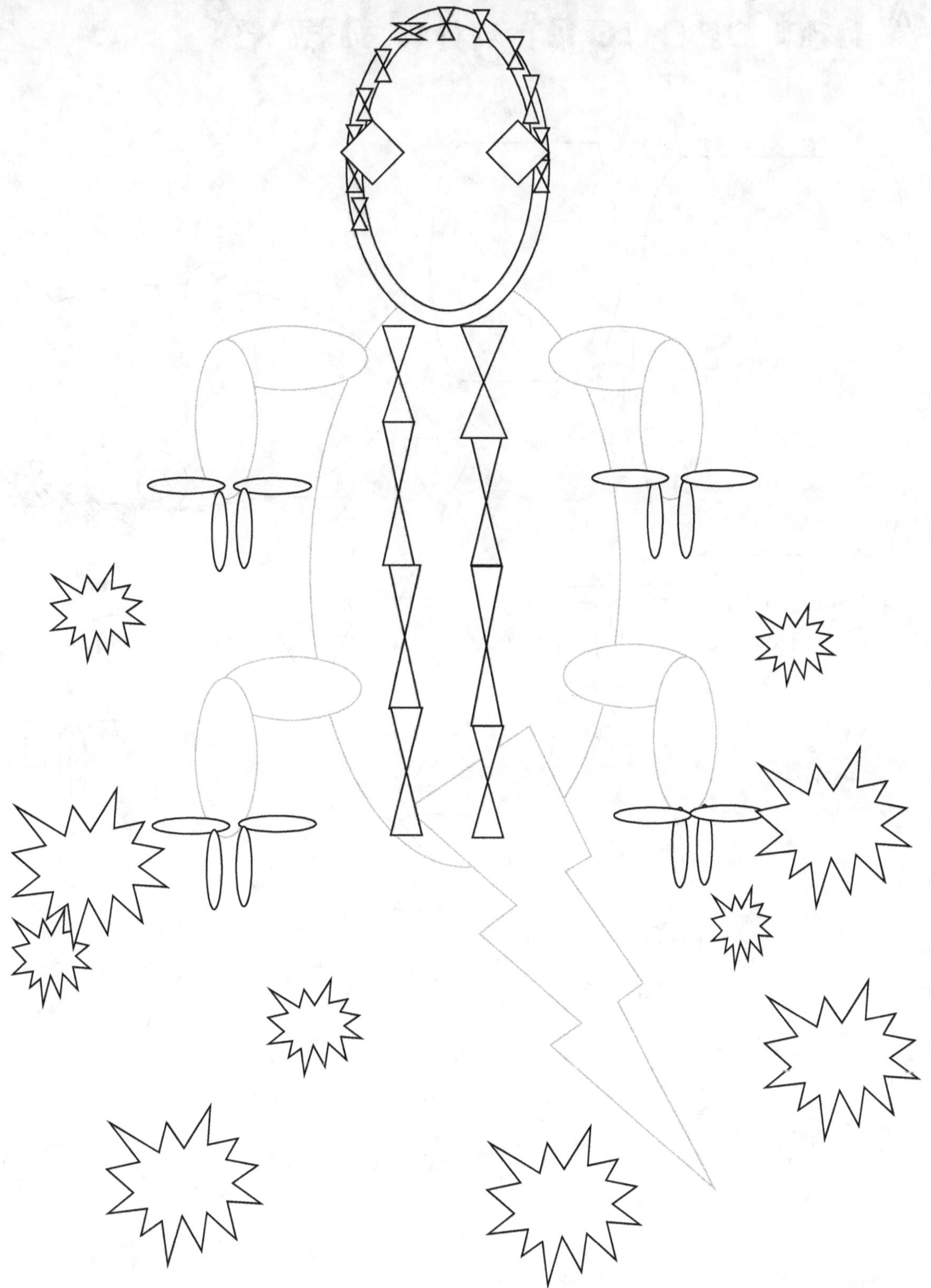

What brought you here?

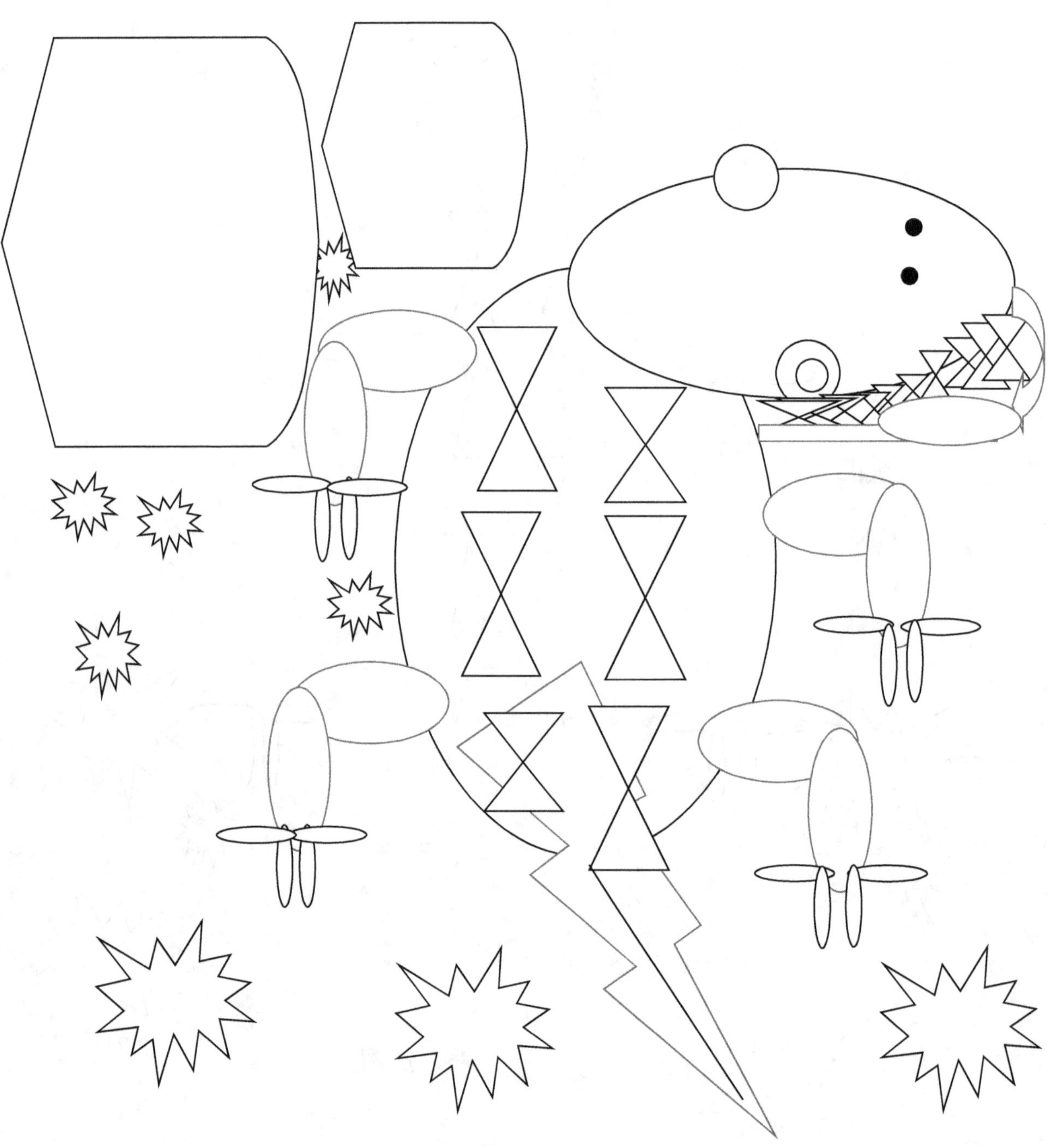

I want to swim.

I love to swim in the ocean too.

I love to swim in the sun every day.

Wait a minute! How many legs do you have?

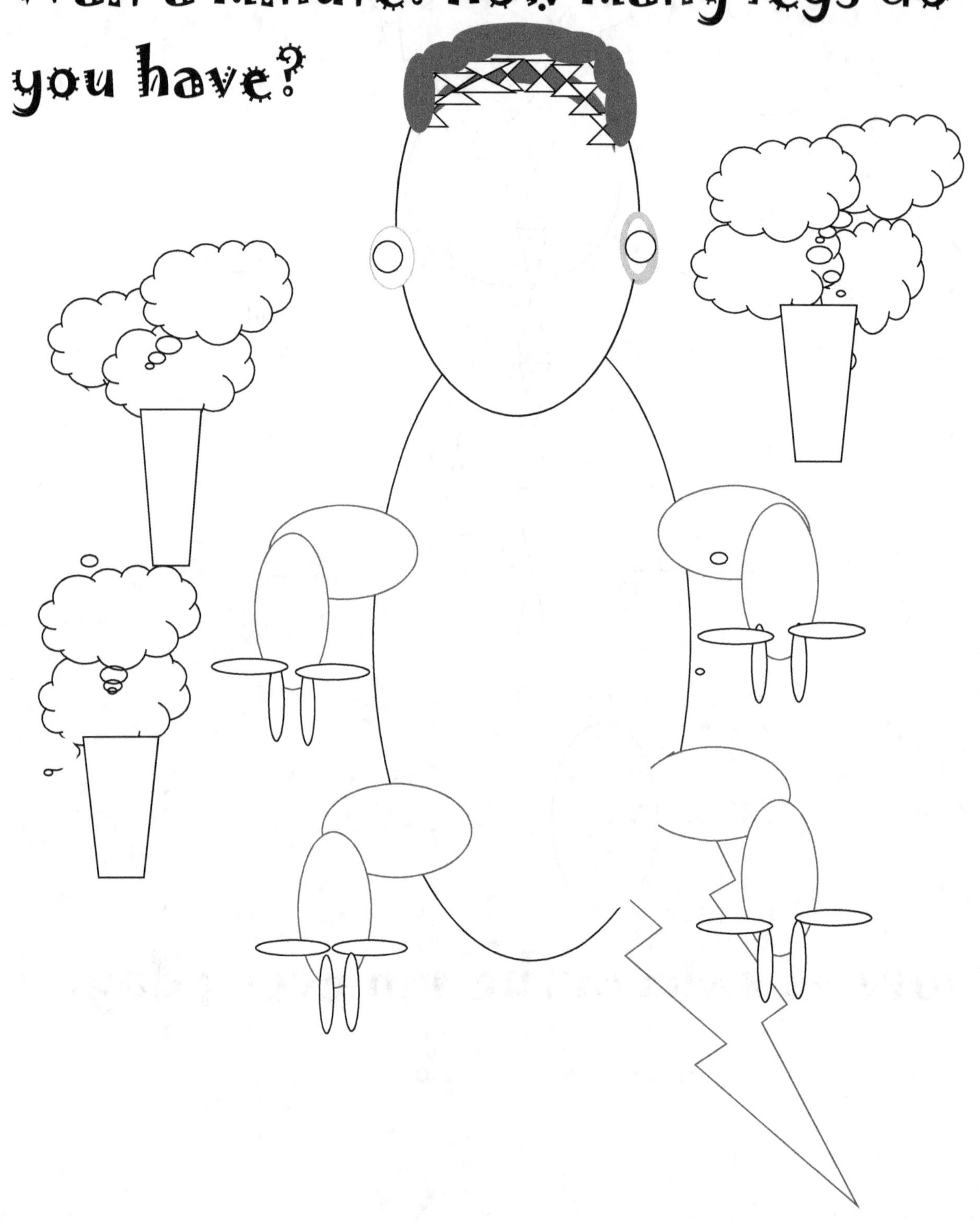

I have four!

I can see two fore legs and two hind legs.

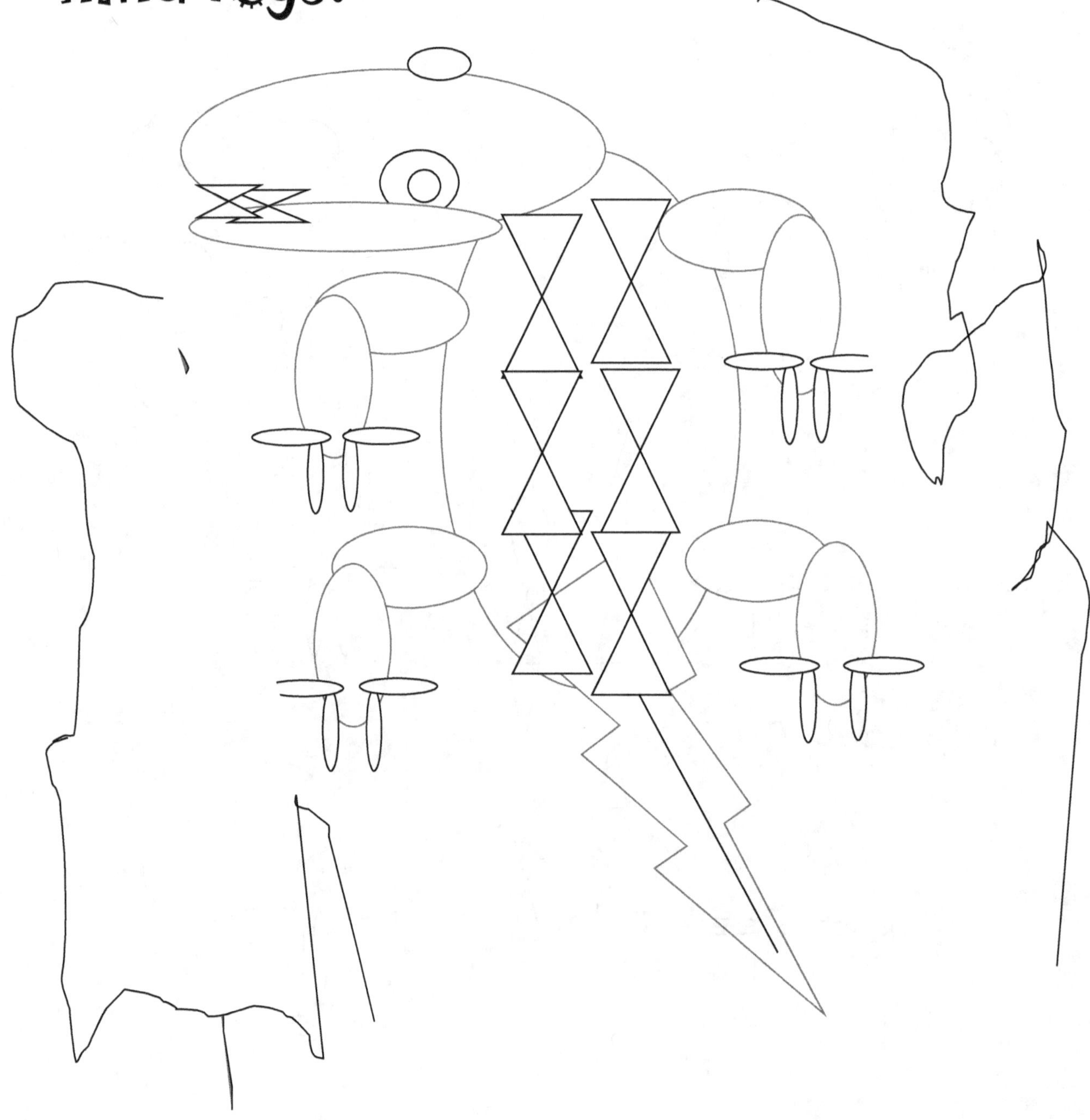

Yes, I have two fore legs and two hind legs just like you!

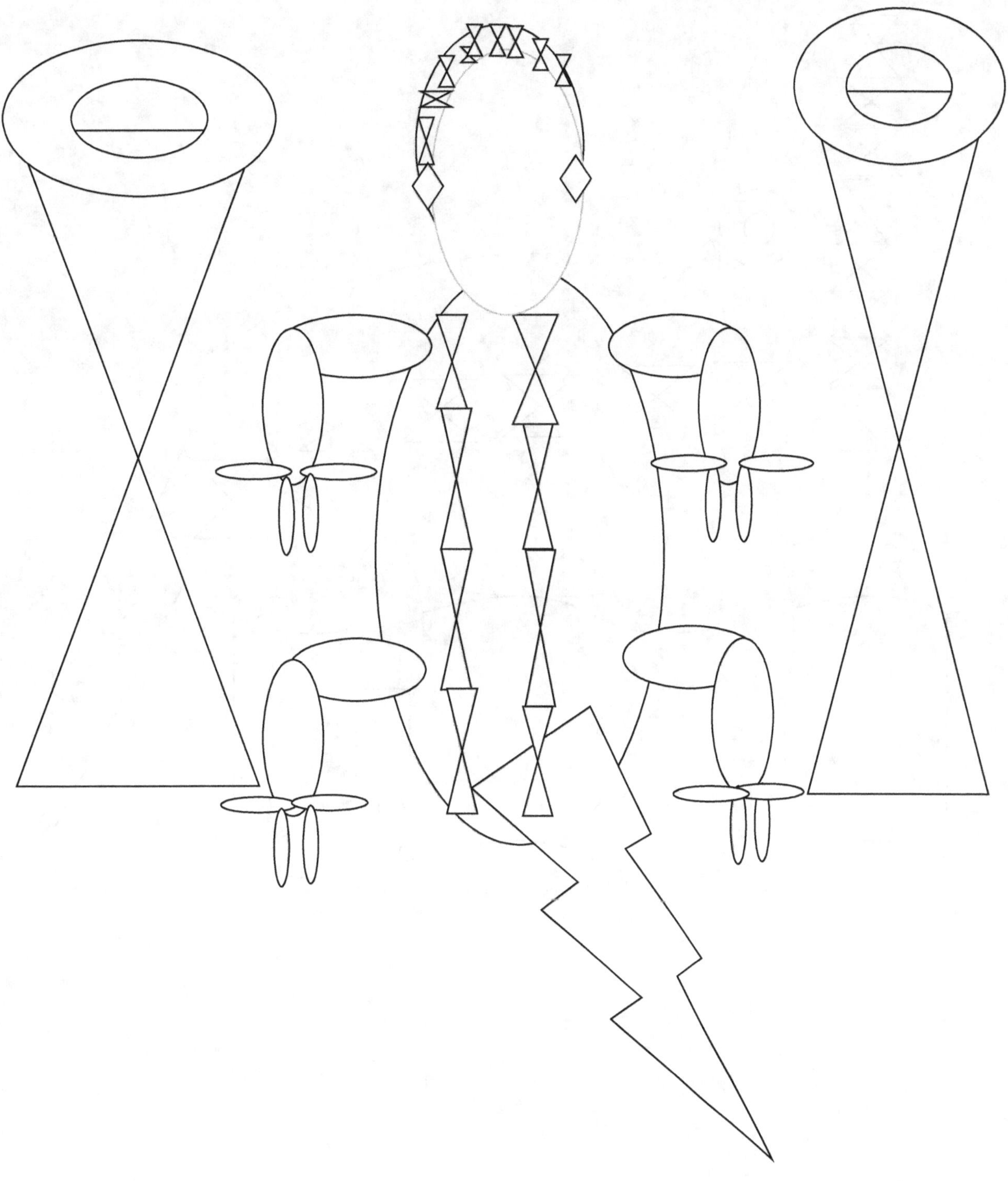

I can crawl on my belly.

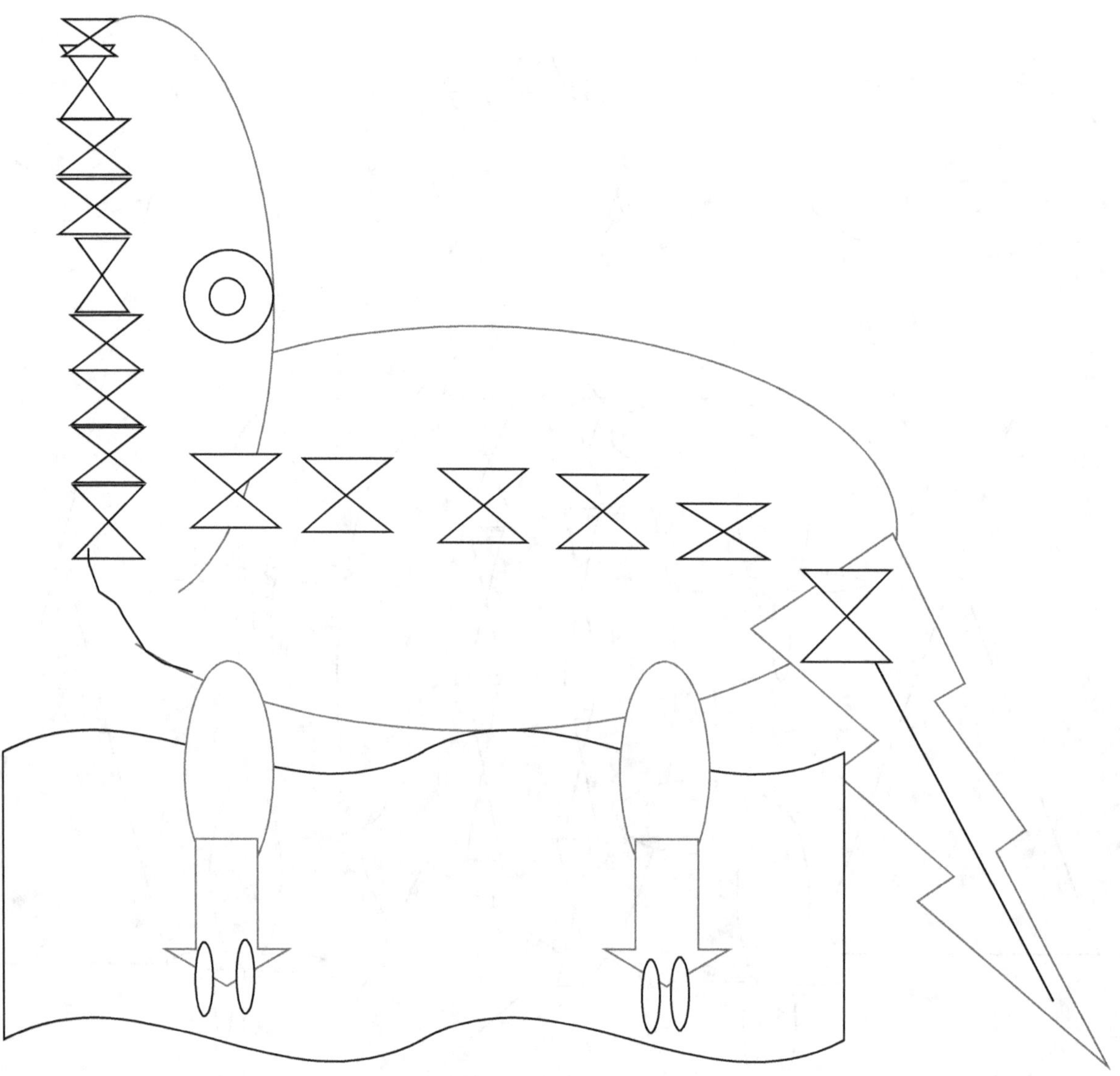

I can crawl on my belly too.

My tail is long and scaly.

My tail is long and scaly too!

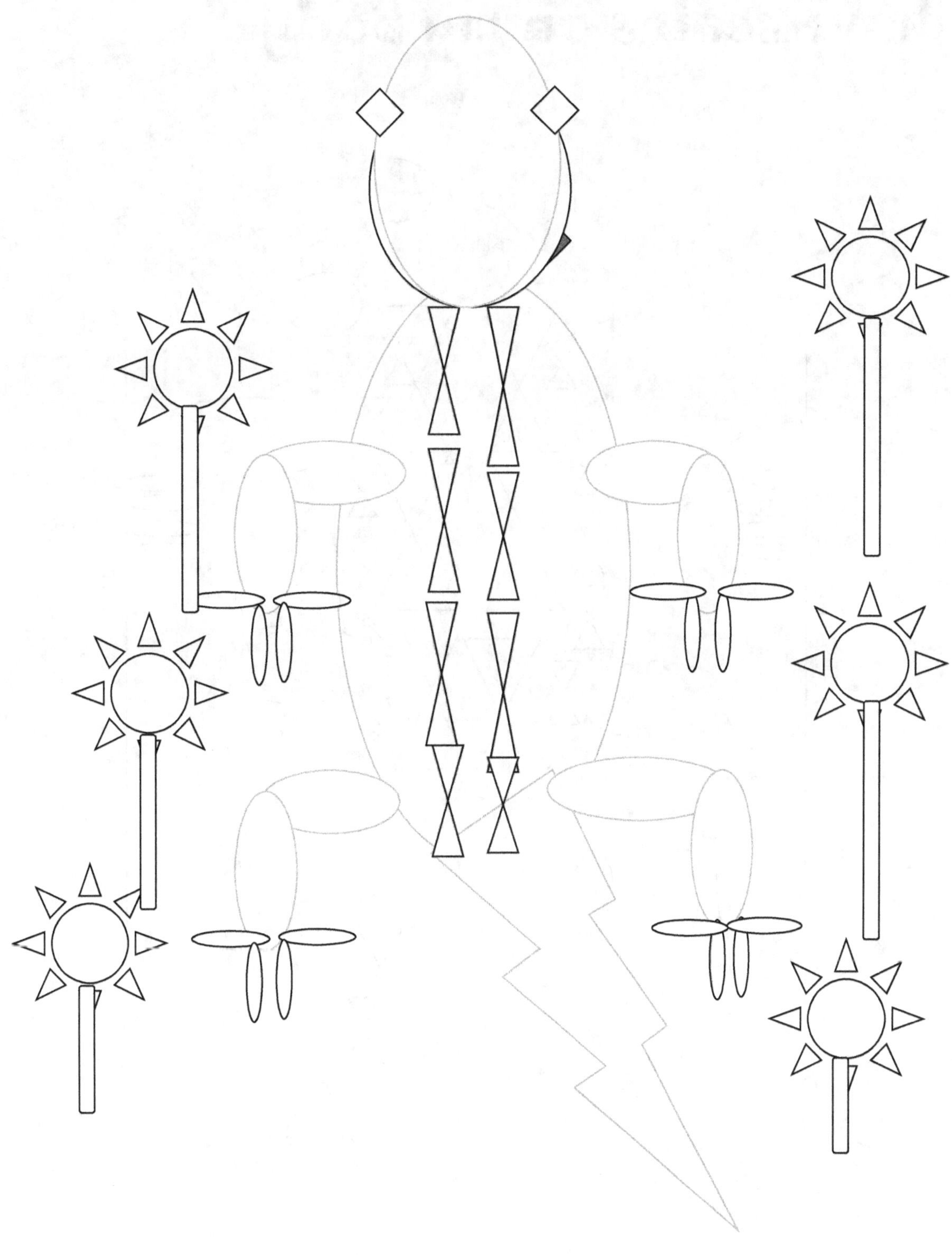

I have scales on my body.

I have scales on my body too!

My teeth are sharp.

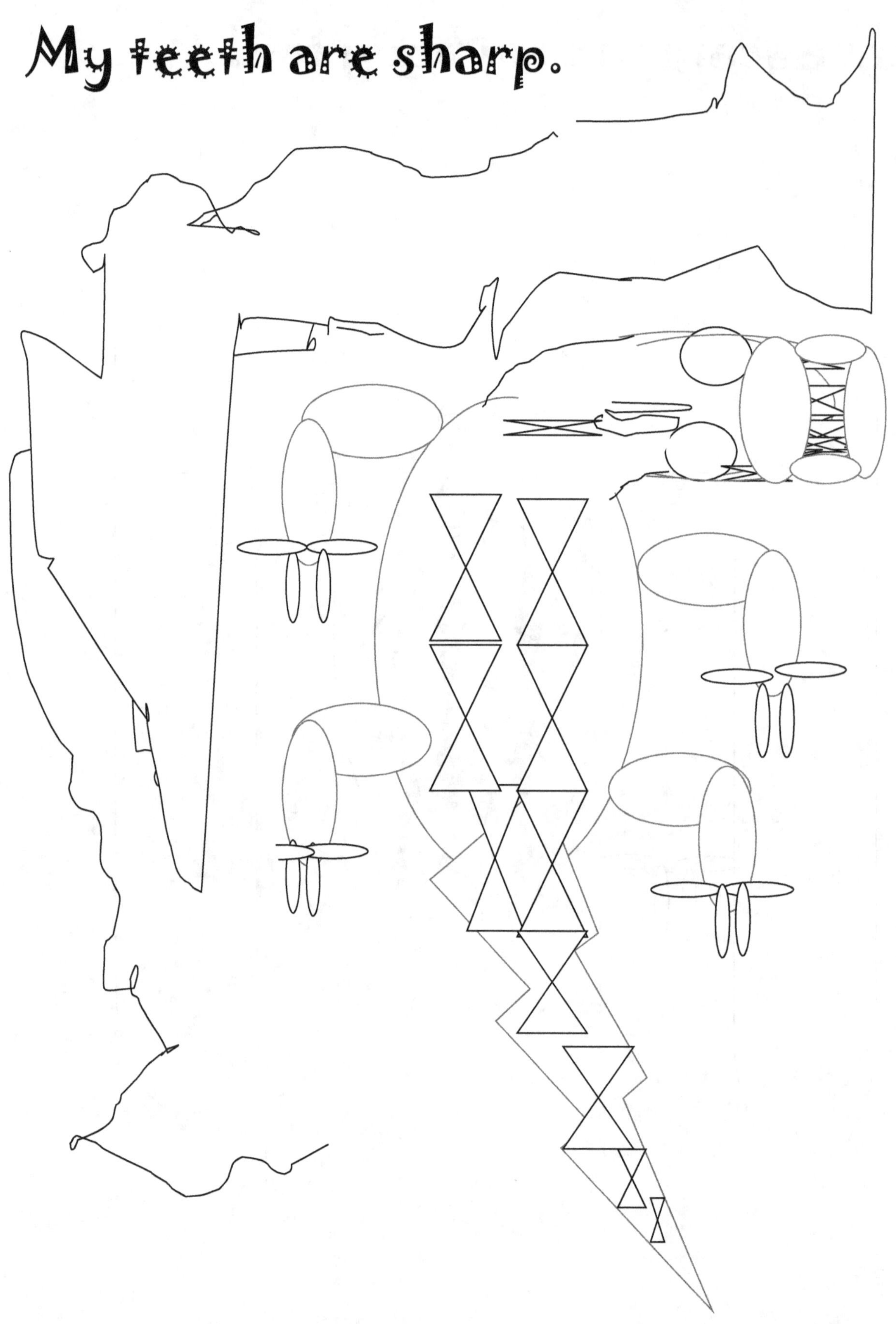

My teeth are sharp too!

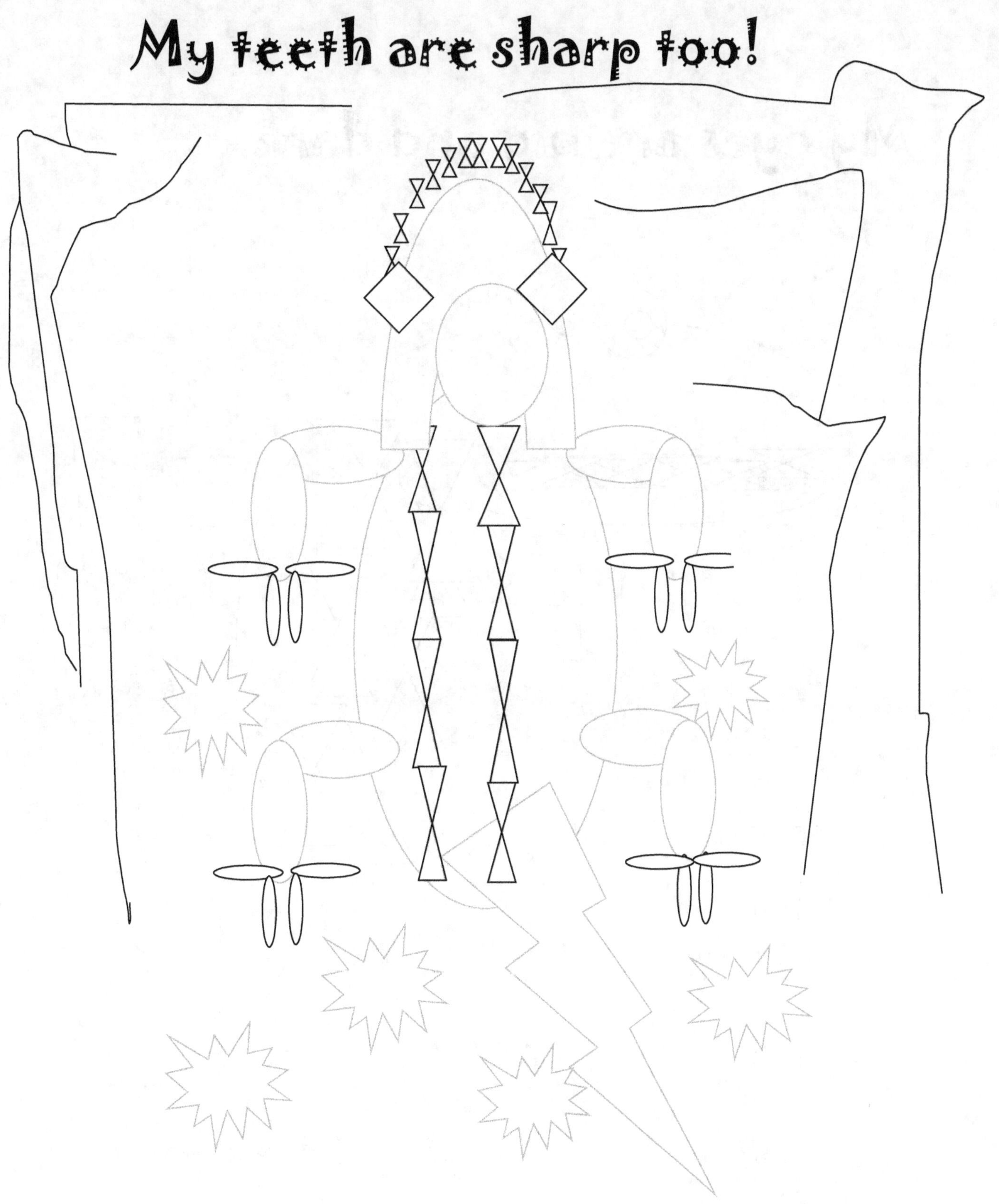

My eyes are big and dark.

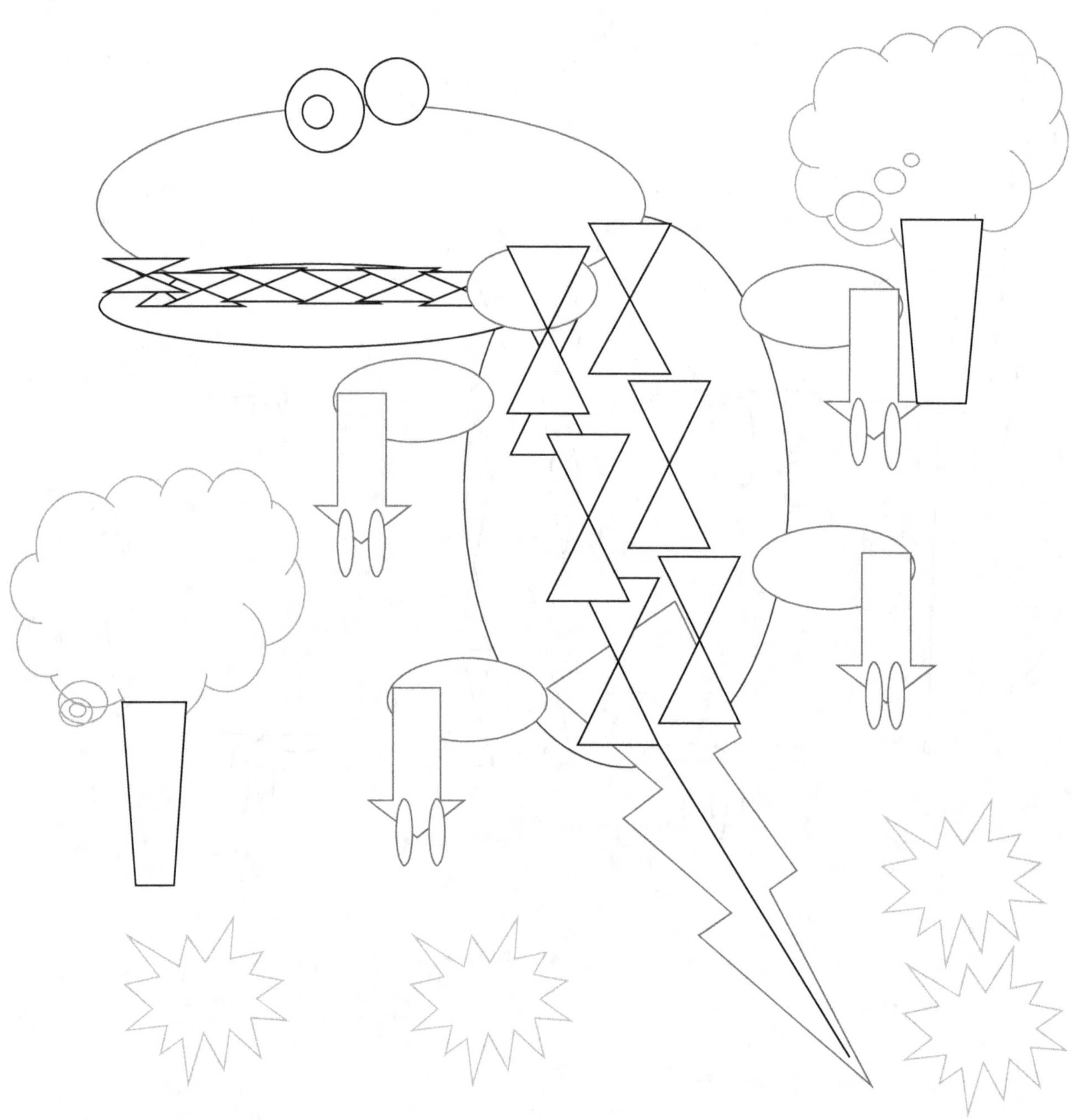

My eyes are big and dark too!

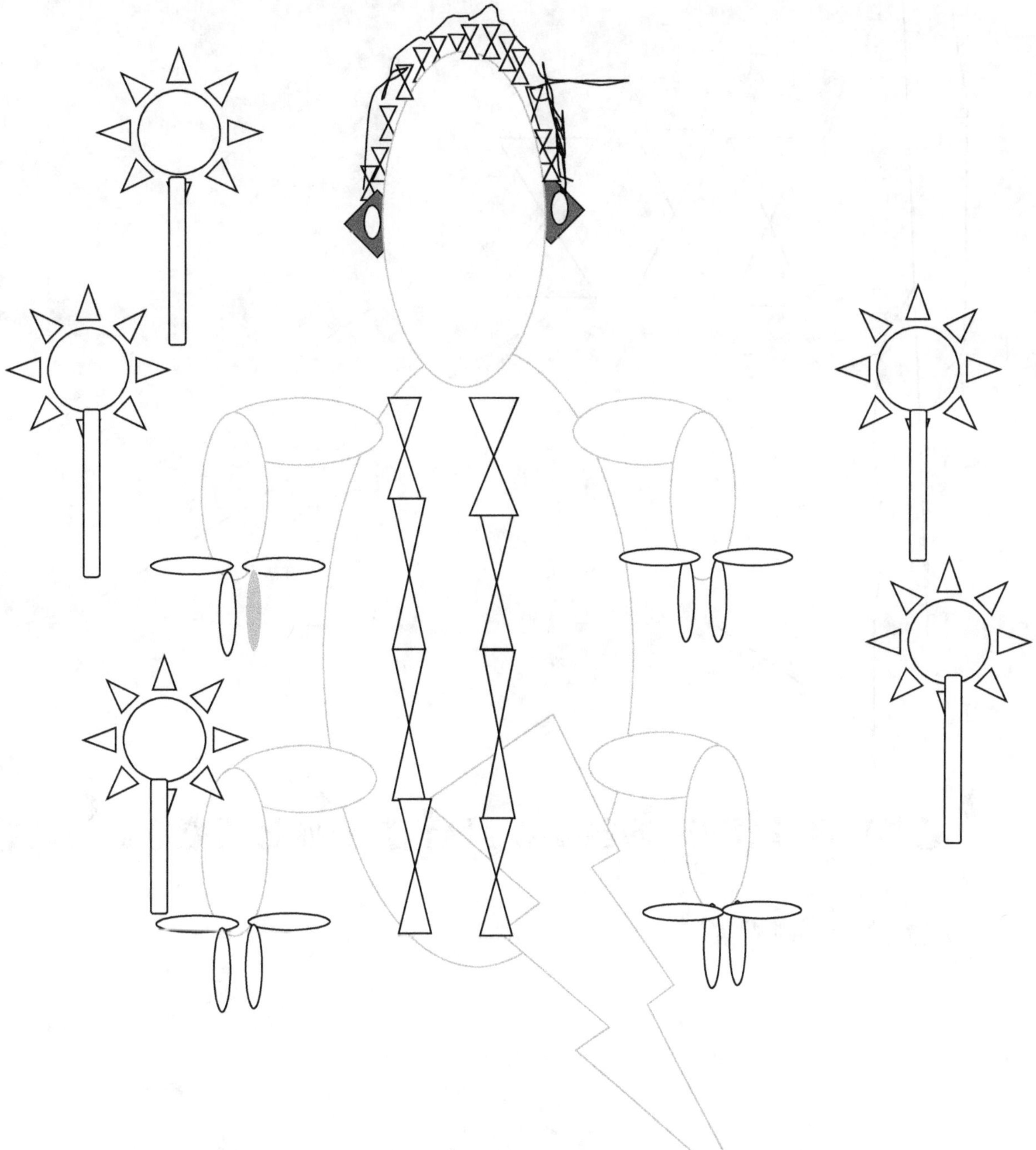

I am going back into the sea. See you later!

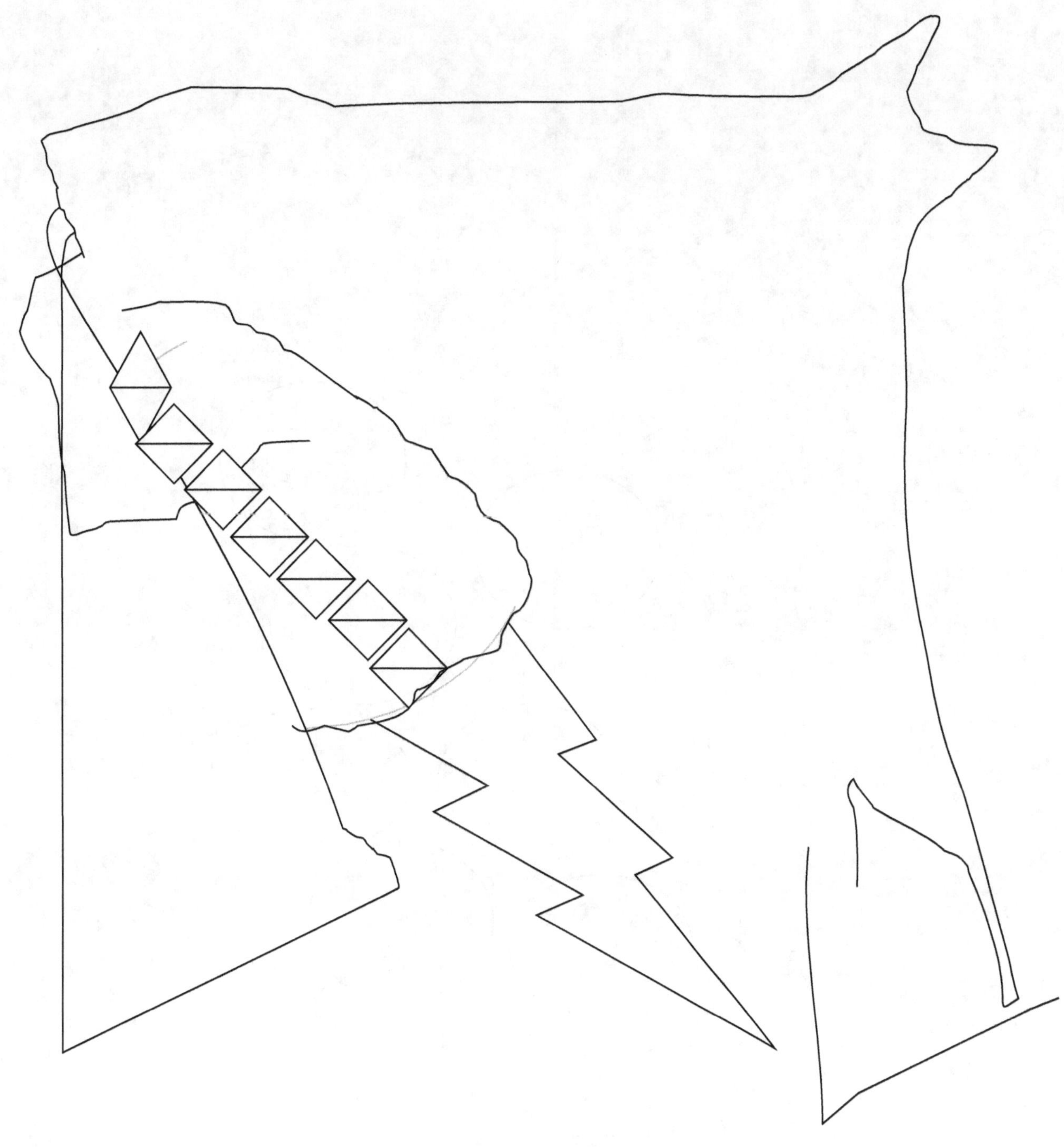

I am going back into the river.
Bye!

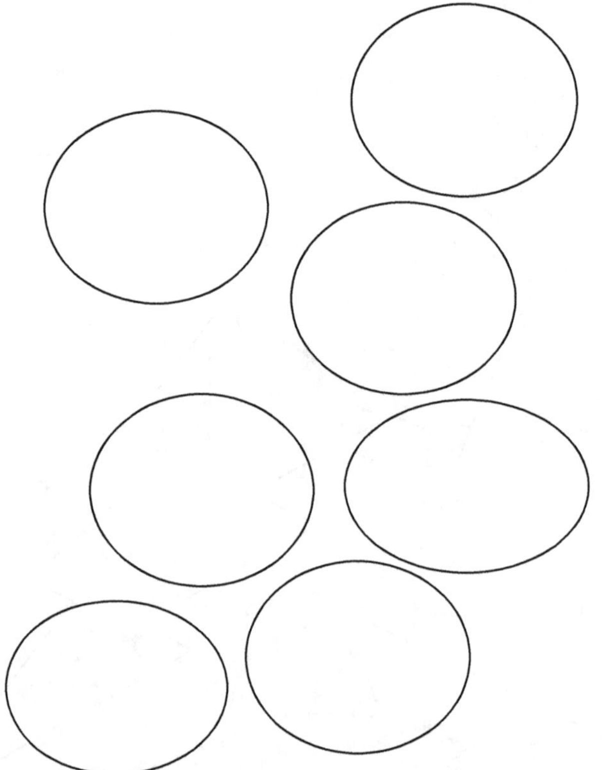

Crocodiles lay eggs.

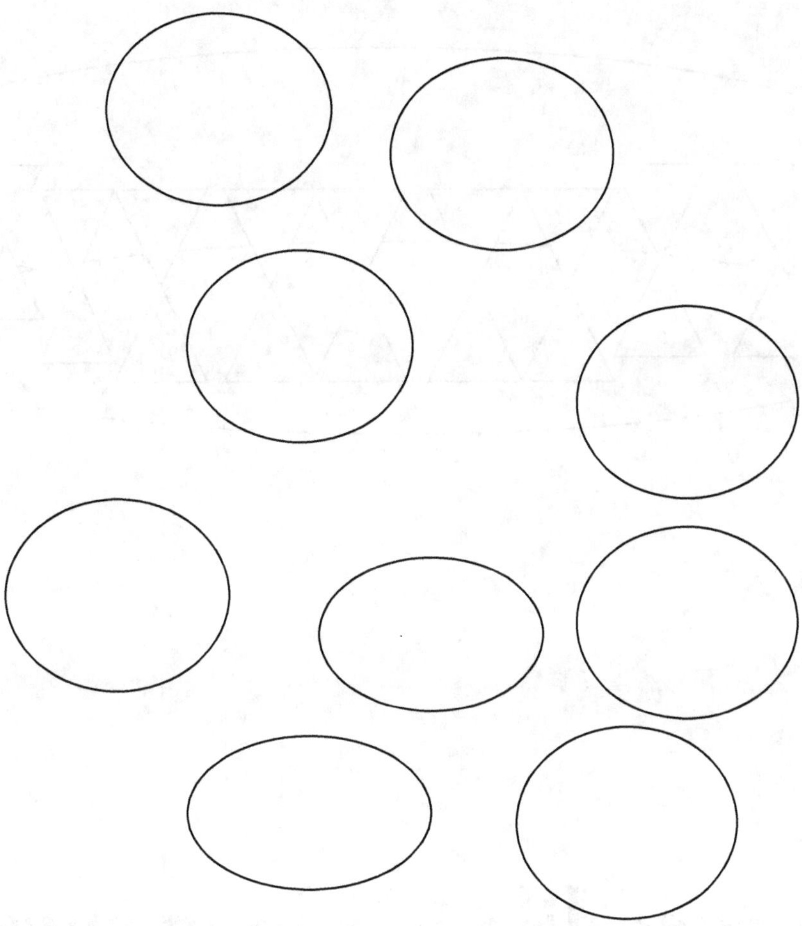

Alligators lay eggs too!

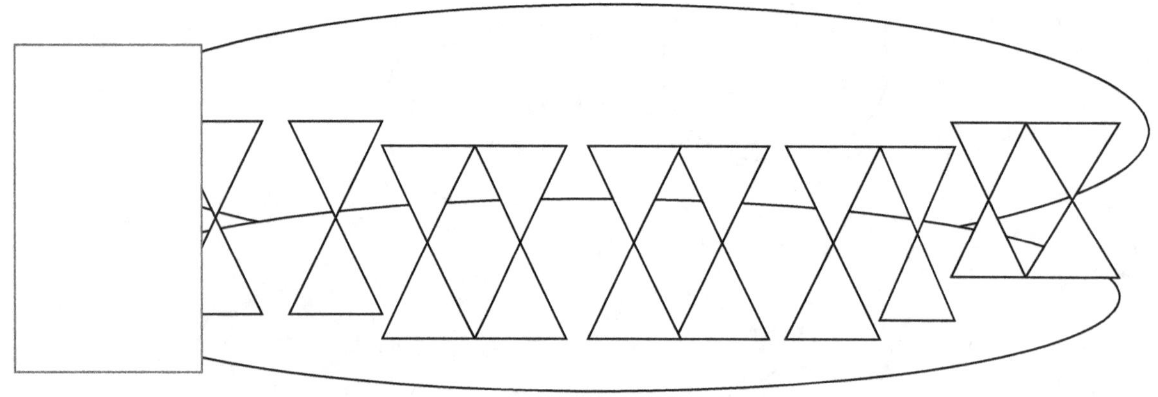

A crocodile has long jaws.

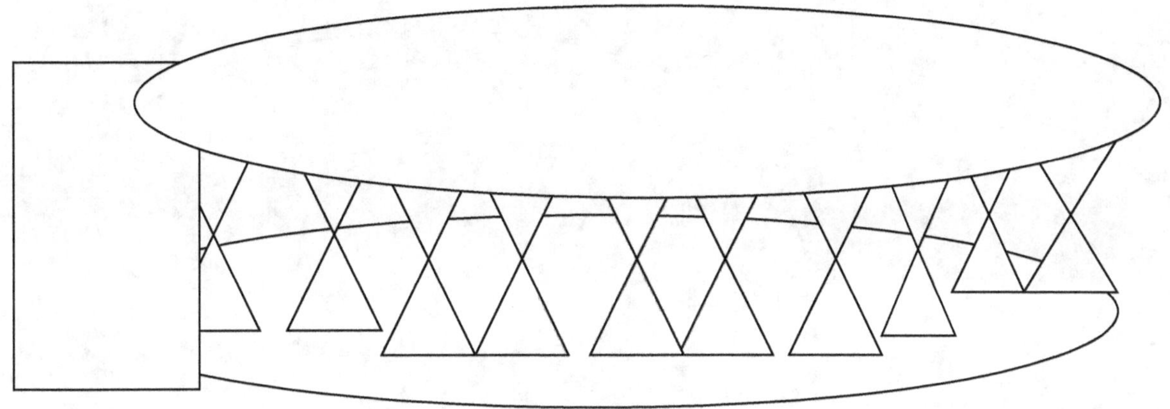

An alligator has long jaws too.

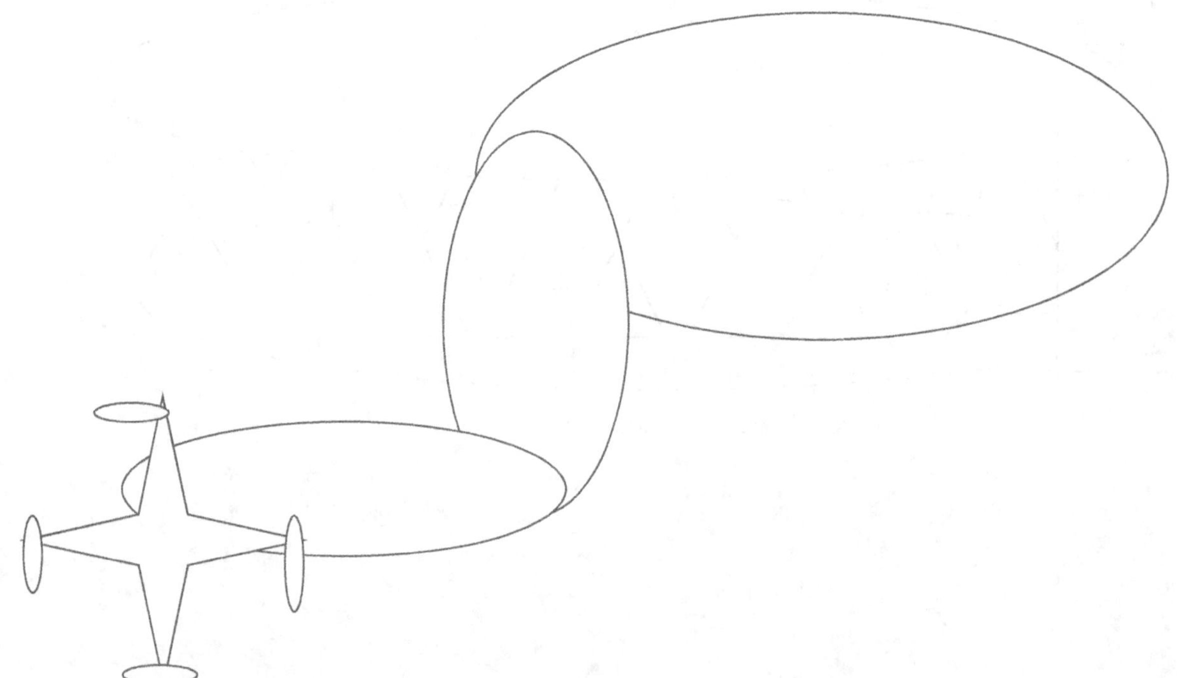

Crocodile's limbs are long.

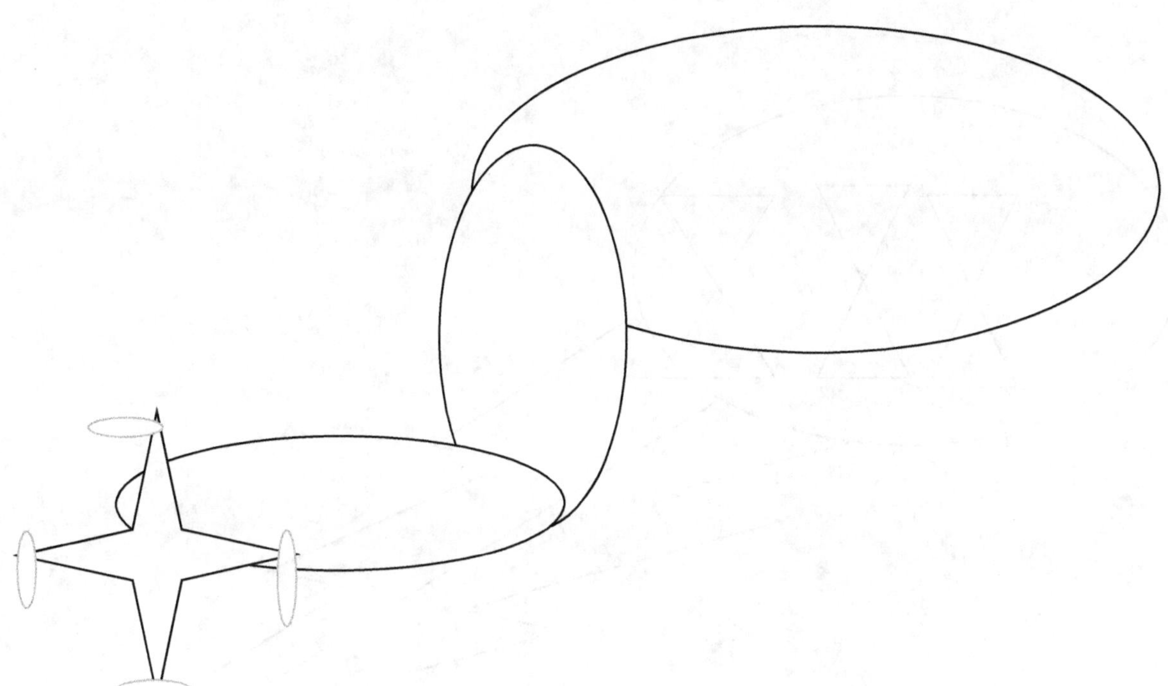

Alligator's limbs are long too!

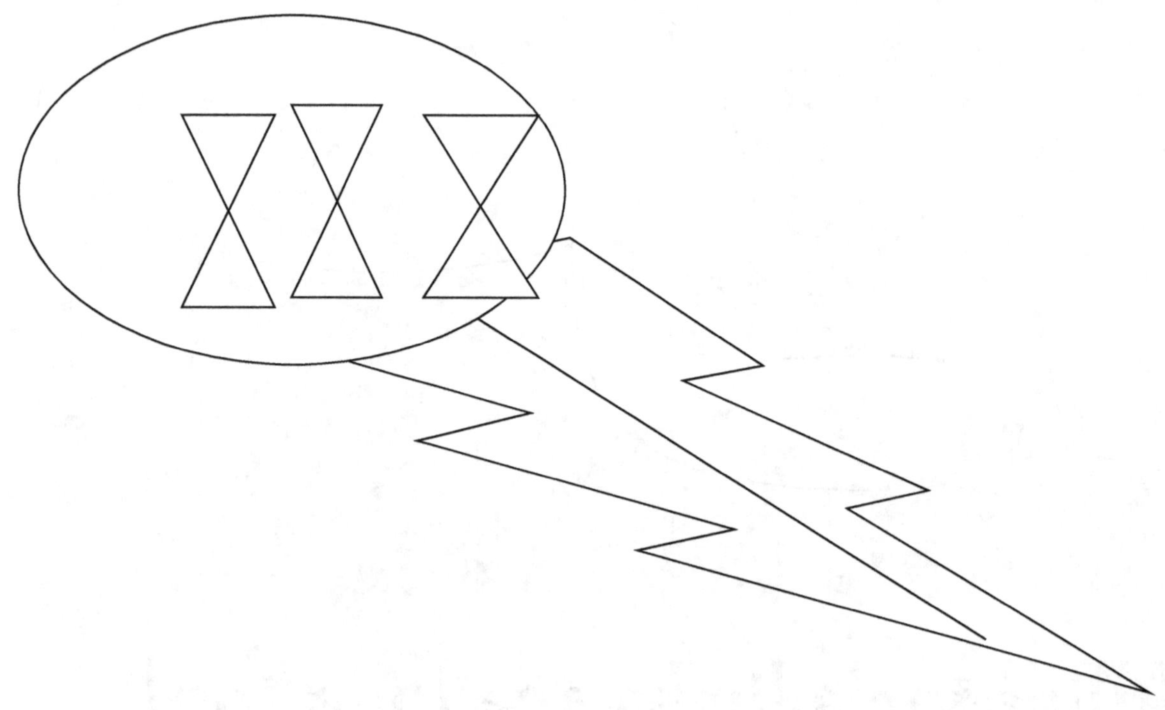

A crocodile has a long tail.

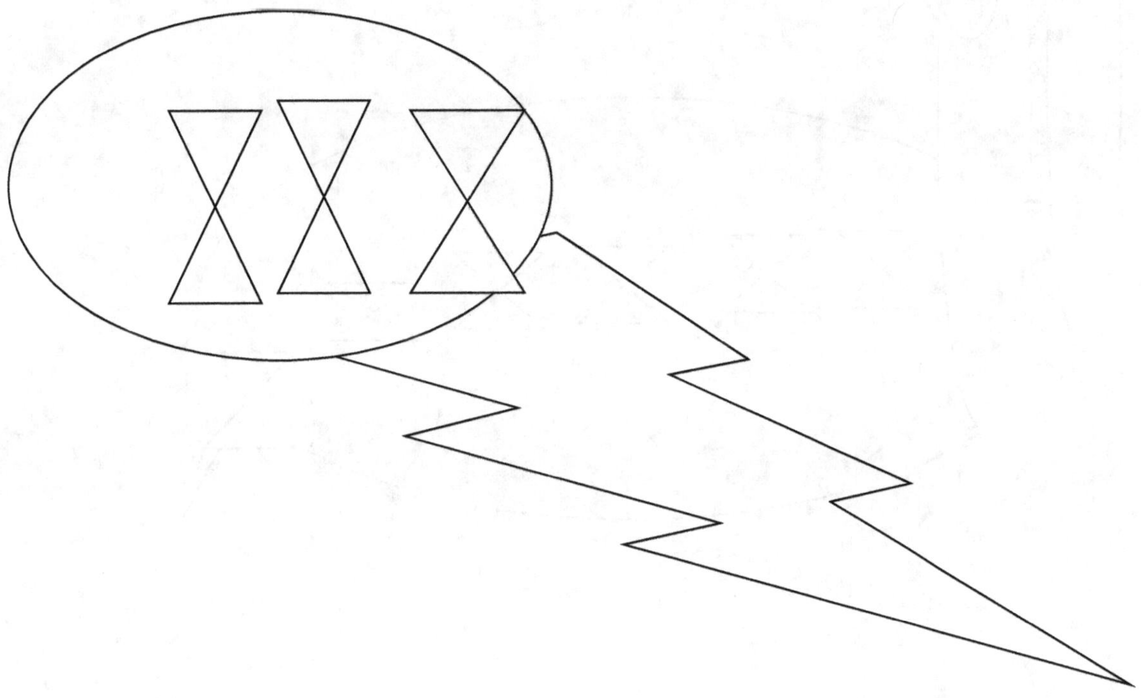

An alligator has a long tail too!

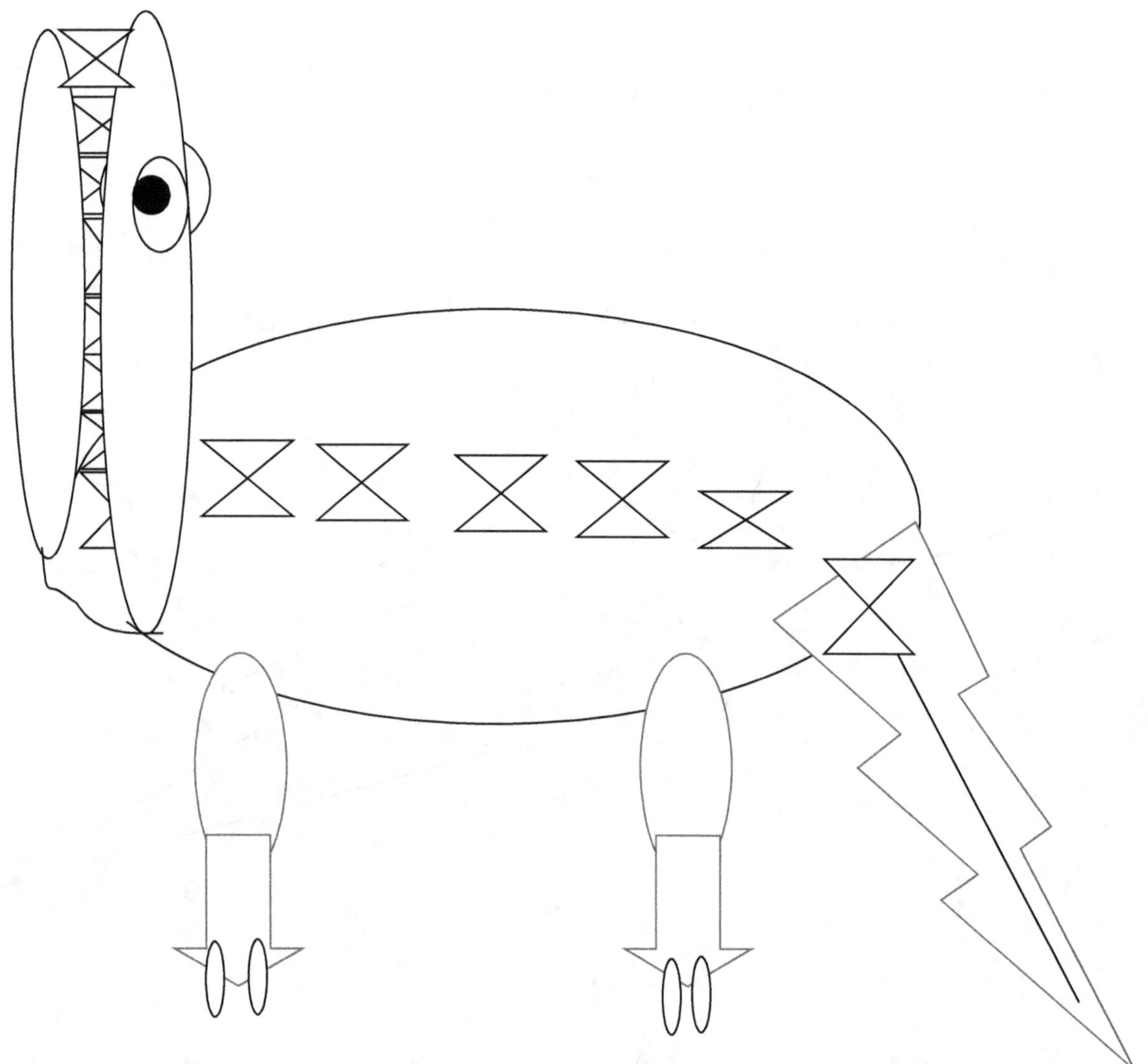

A crocodile is a scary animal.

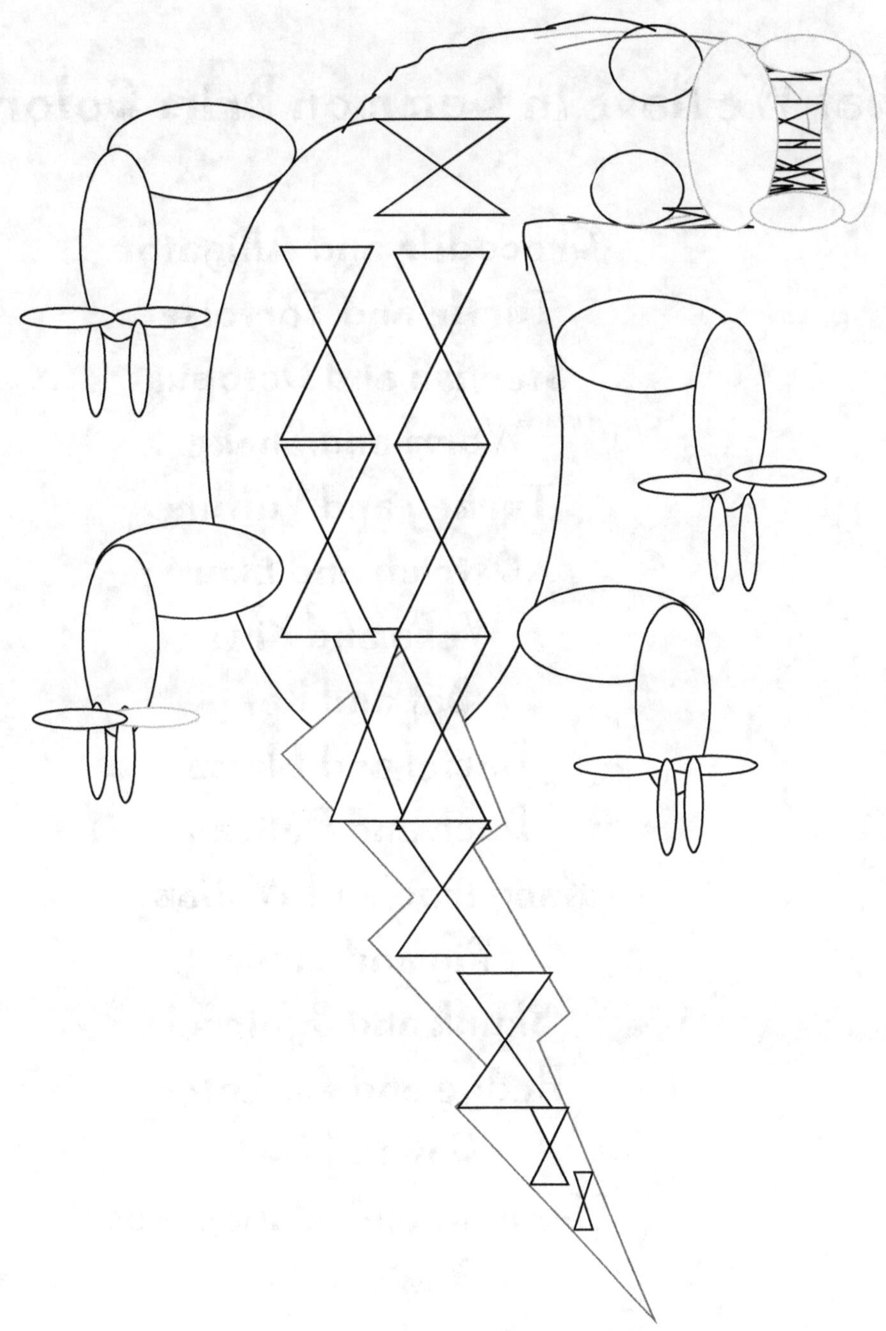

An alligator is scary too!

What We Have in Common Brim Coloring Books

Crocodile and Alligator
Turtle and Tortoise
Starfish and Octopus
Worm and Snake
Turkey and Vulture
Ostrich and Emu
Weka and Kiwi
Bat and Rat
Camel and Llama
Duck and Pelican
Kangaroo and Wallaby
Pig and Tapir
Skunk and Squirrel
Hedge and Anteater
Cat and Owl
Elephant and Rhinoceros
Dog and Fox
Buffalo and Bull
Leopard and Cheetah
Horse and Zebra